Welcome to your very own Yoga Jou

Complete with inspirational and motivational quotes at the top of each page, I hope that you find calm and tranquility while using this journal.

Writing, Ideas, Notetaking, Diary Entries, Planning, Organizing, To-Do Lists, Mind-Maps.
The Choice is Yours. Enjoy.

All work in 'My Yoga Journal Notebook' is copyright and owned by;
Name: ....
Contact Number: ....
Email: ....

"Calming the mind is yoga. Not just standing on the head."

Swami Satchidananda

"Yoga is 99% practice and 1% theory".

Sri Krishna Pattabhi Jois

"Yoga is not about touching your toes. It is what you learn on the way down."

Jigar Gor

"The nature of yoga is to shine the light of awareness
into the darkest corners of the body."
Jason Crandell

"Take care of your body, it's the only place you have to live".

Jim Rohn

"Do not feel lonely. The entire universe is inside of you."

Rumi

"Yoga is a way of moving into stillness in order to experience the truth of who you are."
Erich Schiffmann

"The future depends on what we do in the present."
Mahatma Gandhi

"The pose begins when you want to get out of it."
Baron Baptiste

"Yoga takes you into the present moment. The only place where life exists."

Unknown

"Yoga is invigoration in relaxation. Freedom in routine. Confidence through self-control. Energy within and energy without."

Ymber Delecto

"There is always room for change, but you have to be open to that change."

Kathryn Budig

yoga

"Yoga means addition – addition of energy, strength
and beauty to body, mind and soul."

Amit Ray

"You will never influence the world by trying to be like it."

Unknown

"Go confidently in the direction of your dreams. Live the life you have imagined."

Henry James Thoreau

"There is only one corner of the universe you can be certain of improving, and that's your own self."
Aldous Huxley

"Every moment is a fresh beginning."

T.S. Eliot

"A photographer gets people to pose for him. A yoga instructor gets people to pose for themselves."

T. Guillemet

"True meditation is about being fully present with everything that is—including discomfort and challenges. It is not an escape from life."
Craig Hamilton

"I close my eyes in order to see."
Paul Gauguin

"The body is your temple. Keep it pure and clean for the soul to reside in."

B.K.S Iyengar

"You are never too old to set another goal or to dream a new dream."

C.S. Lewis

"Inhale the future. Exhale the past."

Unknown

"Yoga is the journey of the self, through the self, to the self."

The Bhagavad Gita

"Most people have no idea how good their body is designed to feel."

Kevin Trudeau

"Calming the mind is yoga. Not just standing on the head."

Swami Satchidananda

"Yoga is 99% practice and 1% theory".

Sri Krishna Pattabhi Jois

"Yoga is not about touching your toes. It is what you learn on the way down."

Jigar Gor

"The nature of yoga is to shine the light of awareness into the darkest corners of the body."

Jason Crandell

"Take care of your body, it's the only place you have to live".

Jim Rohn

"Do not feel lonely. The entire universe is inside of you."

Rumi

"Yoga is a way of moving into stillness in order to experience the truth of who you are."
Erich Schiffmann

"The future depends on what we do in the present."
Mahatma Gandhi

"The pose begins when you want to get out of it."
Baron Baptiste

"Yoga takes you into the present moment. The only place where life exists."

Unknown

"Yoga is invigoration in relaxation. Freedom in routine. Confidence through self-control. Energy within and energy without."

Ymber Delecto

"There is always room for change, but you have to be open to that change."

Kathryn Budig

"Yoga means addition – addition of energy, strength and beauty to body, mind and soul."

Amit Ray

"You will never influence the world by trying to be like it."

Unknown

"Go confidently in the direction of your dreams. Live the life you have imagined."

Henry James Thoreau

"There is only one corner of the universe you can be certain of improving, and that's your own self."
Aldous Huxley

"Every moment is a fresh beginning."

T.S. Eliot

"A photographer gets people to pose for him. A yoga instructor gets people to pose for themselves."

T. Guillemet

"True meditation is about being fully present with everything that is—including discomfort and challenges. It is not an escape from life."

Craig Hamilton

"I close my eyes in order to see."
Paul Gauguin

"The body is your temple. Keep it pure and clean for the soul to reside in."

B.K.S Iyengar

"You are never too old to set another goal or to dream a new dream."

C.S. Lewis

"Inhale the future. Exhale the past."

Unknown

"Yoga is the journey of the self, through the self, to the self."

The Bhagavad Gita

"Most people have no idea how good their body is designed to feel."

Kevin Trudeau

"Calming the mind is yoga. Not just standing on the head."

Swami Satchidananda

"Yoga is 99% practice and 1% theory".

Sri Krishna Pattabhi Jois

"Yoga is not about touching your toes. It is what you learn on the way down."

Jigar Gor

"The nature of yoga is to shine the light of awareness into the darkest corners of the body."

Jason Crandell

"Take care of your body, it's the only place you have to live".

Jim Rohn

"Do not feel lonely. The entire universe is inside of you."

Rumi

"Yoga is a way of moving into stillness in order to experience the truth of who you are."
Erich Schiffmann

"The future depends on what we do in the present."
Mahatma Gandhi

"The pose begins when you want to get out of it."
Baron Baptiste

"Yoga takes you into the present moment. The only place where life exists."

Unknown

"Yoga is invigoration in relaxation. Freedom in routine. Confidence through self-control. Energy within and energy without."

Ymber Delecto

"There is always room for change, but you have to be open to that change."

Kathryn Budig

"Yoga means addition – addition of energy, strength and beauty to body, mind and soul."

Amit Ray

"You will never influence the world by trying to be like it."

Unknown

"Go confidently in the direction of your dreams. Live the life you have imagined."
Henry James Thoreau

"There is only one corner of the universe you can be
certain of improving, and that's your own self."

Aldous Huxley

"Every moment is a fresh beginning."

T.S. Eliot

"A photographer gets people to pose for him. A yoga instructor gets people to pose for themselves."

T. Guillemet

"True meditation is about being fully present with everything that is—including discomfort and challenges. It is not an escape from life."
                                        Craig Hamilton

"I close my eyes in order to see."
Paul Gauguin

"The body is your temple. Keep it pure and clean for the soul to reside in."

B.K.S Iyengar

"You are never too old to set another goal or to dream a new dream."

C.S. Lewis

"Inhale the future. Exhale the past."
Unknown

"Yoga is the journey of the self, through the self, to the self."

The Bhagavad Gita

"Most people have no idea how good their body is designed to feel."

Kevin Trudeau

"Calming the mind is yoga. Not just standing on the head."

Swami Satchidananda

"Yoga is 99% practice and 1% theory".

Sri Krishna Pattabhi Jois

"Yoga is not about touching your toes. It is what you
learn on the way down."

Jigar Gor

"The nature of yoga is to shine the light of awareness
into the darkest corners of the body."

Jason Crandell

"Take care of your body, it's the only place you have to live".

Jim Rohn

"Do not feel lonely. The entire universe is inside of you."

Rumi

"Yoga is a way of moving into stillness in order to experience the truth of who you are."
Erich Schiffmann

"The future depends on what we do in the present."
Mahatma Gandhi

"The pose begins when you want to get out of it."
Baron Baptiste

"Yoga takes you into the present moment. The only place where life exists."

Unknown

"Yoga is invigoration in relaxation. Freedom in routine. Confidence through self-control. Energy within and energy without."

Ymber Delecto

"There is always room for change, but you have to be open to that change."

Kathryn Budig

_____

_____

_____

_____

_____

_____

_____

_____

_____

_____

_____

_____

_____

_____

_____

_____

_____

"Yoga means addition – addition of energy, strength and beauty to body, mind and soul."

Amit Ray

"You will never influence the world by trying to be like it."

Unknown

YOGA

"Go confidently in the direction of your dreams. Live the life you have imagined."
Henry James Thoreau

"There is only one corner of the universe you can be certain of improving, and that's your own self."
Aldous Huxley

"Every moment is a fresh beginning."

T.S. Eliot

"A photographer gets people to pose for him. A yoga instructor gets people to pose for themselves."

T. Guillemet

"True meditation is about being fully present with everything that is—including discomfort and challenges. It is not an escape from life."

Craig Hamilton

"I close my eyes in order to see."
Paul Gauguin

"The body is your temple. Keep it pure and clean for the soul to reside in."

B.K.S Iyengar

"You are never too old to set another goal or to dream a new dream."

C.S. Lewis

I ♥ yoga

"Inhale the future. Exhale the past."

Unknown

"Yoga is the journey of the self, through the self, to the self."

The Bhagavad Gita

"Most people have no idea how good their body is designed to feel."

Kevin Trudeau

Thank you for using this Yoga Journal Notebook.

Your Comments and Feedback are highly appreciated. If you would like to leave a Review with Amazon, please find the link to this Journal. Click and scroll down to where you will be able to leave a review.

Thank you in advance, I look forward to hearing from you.

Freya Carter

Made in the USA
Middletown, DE
06 April 2024

52676563R00057